Shifting Gears

Catapulting Your Life to the Next Level

Table of Contents

The only limit to the height of your achievements is the reach of your dreams and your willingness to work for them.

— Michelle Obama

Chapter 1. Introduction

Embark on an invigorating journey packed with wisdom nuggets, transformational insights, and attainment strategies with our Special Report - "Shifting Gears: Catapulting Your Life to the Next Level." This lively report is your roadmap to break free from mediocrity and launch into a realm of excellence and fulfillment. Brimming with easy-to-implement tactics, inspiring case studies, and scientifically backed facts, it guides you toward harnessing your potentials, bolstering your self-confidence, and crafting the life you've always dreamed about. Finding your inner strength, mapping your path towards success, igniting that dormant spark, it's all within reach, and it starts here. Embrace the uplifting journey awaiting you - buckle up and shift gears towards the next level of your life unimaginable! It's time to unlock your future and bask in the vibrant colors of success, purpose, and happiness. This special report is more than just a purchase; it's your passport to a life of limitless possibilities!

Chapter 2. Recognizing Your Current State: A Self-Assessment

Nestled within the depths of your being, there lies a dormant seed - the potential for greatness that's waiting to bloom. The first step towards tiredly tapping into this dormant potential is an authentic and fearless gaze into your current self. This panoramic snapshot of where you are standing at present, is the foundation upon which your journey to greatness is about to unfold. So, let's dive right in.

2.1. The Power of Self-Assessment

Perception, they say, is indeed reality. The lens through which we view ourselves and our circumstances dramatically impacts all facets of our life. Yet, this lens often gets tinted by biases and misconceptions. This is where self-assessment steps in. A robust self-assessment method provides you with an accurate designation of your strengths, weaknesses, passions, and areas you may need to improve upon. More than just a voyage of self-discovery, this process equips you to make more informed decisions, nurture your strengths, and effectively transform your weaknesses into stepping stones for growth.

2.2. Decoding The Inner Self: Strengths And Weaknesses

Self-assessment, in essence, is an in-depth exploration of your character traits, personal values, skills, and passions. Begin by identifying your strengths. Reflect on the times when you felt the most euphoria or satisfaction. Ask yourself, "What skills or attributes were I using then?" Your strengths could range from leadership, communication, or creative thinking to resilience, adaptability, or emotional intelligence.

Next, pinpoint your weaknesses or areas of improvement. It's not about criticism but understanding. Recognize patterns where you find yourself struggling or feeling uncomfortable. Acknowledge these areas without any self-reproach. Remember, by doing so, you are already on your path to improvement!

2.3. The Capacity To Change: Identifying Habits And Patterns

More often than we care to admit, our habits bear a significant influence on our daily lives. They can either be the pillars supporting our success or the chains holding us back. Identifying these patterns and their implications allows us to consciously decide whether they serve our aspirations or not. Start by noting the habits that make up your day, both positive and negative. Reflect on why they exist and how they impact your life.

2.4. The Aspirations Cue: Pinpointing Passions And Goals

Equally important as understanding where you are now, is having clarity about where you want to be. These ideal scenes often stem from our passions and goals. Start by asking yourself, "What are the activities, tasks, or sectors that truly ignite my passion?" Following this, outline your long-term and short-term goals. These could be related to your career, personal development, relationships, health, or lifestyle. It's essential to clarify these goals and ensure their alignment with your passions.

2.5. Reflective Journaling: Guided Self-Assessment Practice

One of the most effective and powerful self-assessment tools is reflective journaling. The act of putting ideas onto paper can stimulate insights that might remain elusive in thought alone. Dedicate a section of your journal to each aspect of this self-assessment. Write your strengths, weaknesses, habits, passions, and goals. Be honest, be creative, yet be thoughtful.

While this journey may seem challenging initially, as a seeming Pandora's box of self-doubt, naivety, and potentiality, persist. This journey of self-assessment, while a pathway into your deeper being, is only the first page of the grand novel of self-discovery, self-awareness, and self-mastery waiting to be written by you. As you patiently and diligently navigate this chapter, remember, your exploration is building the most robust foundation for all your future endeavors.

Chapter 3. The Power of Mindset: Cultivating a Growth Attitude

Enveloped within each of us is a potent force—an unseen driver that navigates the contours of our collective consciousness and our individual identities. This force fuels our actions, mirrors our beliefs, and crafts our reality. Cloaked under the name of 'mindset,' this force, so significantly essential and yet so profoundly underestimated, acts as the steadfast anchor or the sprightly helium balloon in our journey toward fulfillment.

3.1. The Two Tide-turning Mindsets

Be it navigating the mundane or maneuvering the extraordinary, two significant mindsets influence our thoughts, actions, and ultimately, our lives: the Fixed Mindset and the Growth Mindset.

Existing on the one end of the spectrum is the 'Fixed Mindset.' It manifests in individuals who believe their intelligence and abilities are static, unchangeable traits endowed at birth, and no external effort can bring about a transformation in these innate qualities. A fixed mindset erects invisible boundaries, limits personal and professional growth, and confines people within an echo chamber of self-doubt, self-pity, and at times, self-sabotage.

On the opposite end of the mindset spectrum, there dwells a radically different outlook—the 'Growth Mindset.' This perspective nurtures the belief that intelligence and skill can be developed and improved upon with concerted effort, focus, and perseverance. More than a mental trait, a growth mindset is a way of life that powers exploration, cultivates resilience, and feeds the ceaseless pursuit of excellence.

3.2. The Growth Mindset: Planting the Seeds of Transformation

The adoption of a growth mindset starts with understanding that our abilities, intelligence, and competencies are not fixed but malleable, capable of growth and change. But a growth mindset isn't just about recognizing that we can improve—it's about genuinely wanting to improve, and taking consistent, meaningful steps towards that improvement.

1. Embrace Challenges: Adversity fuels progress. Each challenge is an invitation to stretch your abilities, test your tenacity, and grow beyond your comfort zone.

2. Persist in the face of setbacks: Errors and failures are not definitive dead-ends, but detours forcing reassessment and reinforcing resilience. Each setback provides an opportunity for introspection, learning, and growth.

3. Dedicate to Deliberate Practice: Growth results from consistent, focused practice. Committing to tasks that push your abilities and exercising constructive feedback prepares you for complex challenges and helps master the necessary skills.

4. Emphasize Effort over Outcome: Tangible results may inspire, but it's the intangible effort that empowers and ignites the spirit of persistence.

5. Understand the Value of Constructive Criticism: Criticism, when rendered constructively, can serve as a potent tool for personal betterment and growth. It directs attention to weak spots and encourages strategies for improvement.

3.3. The Catalyst of Change: The Growth Mindset in Action

With roots firmly planted in scientific research, the power of the growth mindset lies in its potential to spur personal and professional development. Paradigm-altering effects encompass building resilience in times of adversity, fostering a love for learning, sparking innovation, and heightening overall life satisfaction.

With the adoption of a growth mindset, the boundary between 'impossible' and 'I'm possible' becomes increasingly blurred, encouraging individuals to overcome hurdles and evolve continually. Constancy in this attitude enables one to not only weather life's storms with grace but also to harness these tempestuous times as powerful learning experiences.

The magnitude of a growth mindset cannot be overstated. From upscaling the professional field's performance levels to fostering personal relationships rooted in understanding and empathy, the growth mindset does not merely exist—it thrives, facilitates, and elevates.

3.4. Conclusion: Fostering a Growth Mindset

Having a growth mindset is a journey, not an end in itself. It's a continuous endeavor, requiring purposeful, consistent effort. It's about reshaping our thought patterns, refining our reactions, and proactively seeking growth opportunities.

In essence, cultivating a growth mindset is not just about facilitating growth—it's about reveling in that growth, savoring the journey as much as, if not more than, the destination. By celebrating the process, the struggle, the effort, we can not only embrace growth but also cherish the lessons and nuances of the journey.

To create a mindset blind to boundaries, deaf to discouragements, and unreceptive to constraints, we need to engulf ourselves in a growth-centric ideology that employs effort as its emissary of excellence and embraces mistakes as the clandestine custodians of growth. So let us welcome this mindset and sweep aside the dust of doubts, allowing the resilient roots of possibility, perseverance, and personal growth to flourish in their pristine glory.

Chapter 4. Visioneering Your Future: Crafting Your Personal Blueprint

This section starts at the precipice of your future, gazing at the broad horizon that lies before you. Each one's life is like an uncharted sea, and our vision is the compass that guides us through our voyages.

4.1. Laying the Foundation: Understanding Your Vision

Before you set about crafting your personal blueprint, it's important to understand the essence of vision. Vision is more than a distant goal. It's a vivid, cogent idea of what the future could hold, embedded firmly with your deepest values and aspirations. It's a purposeful projection of your ideal future designed to inform your decisions and guide your actions. Crafting a clear vision is, in essence, creating a framework for purposeful living.

The interpretation and definition of a vision can be as unique as each individual. You might view it as a targeted career goal, such as becoming a renowned writer or a leading entrepreneur, whereas for another it might be a more personal ambition like leading a life rooted in sustainability and simplicity. No two visions are the same, and that's the beauty of personal blueprints - they're as unique and varied as a fingerprint.

4.2. Starting at Square One: Self-Exploration

For you to design your personal blueprint, it's crucial to immerse yourself in self-exploration. It involves discovering your values, passions, strengths, and weaknesses.

Understanding what resonates with your soul and sparks deep-seated excitement is a fundamental aspect of this exploration. To gather these insights, you might consider evergreen methods like journaling your thoughts, dreams, and ideas consistently or practicing mindfulness meditation to tune into your inner feelings and desires.

Simultaneously, comprehending your character strengths, as well as areas needing improvement, is key to this process. Tools, like the VIA survey or SWOT Analysis, can offer valuable introspective insights that can help you refine your vision strategically.

It's also equally important to take stock of your present situation. Are you deadlocked in a job that brings you no joy? Are your current routines and habits incongruent with your desired future? Answers to such reflective inquiries will serve as a baseline for your forward progress.

4.3. Plotting the Course: Setting Your Vision

After you've painted a thorough and raw picture of your present self, the next step is to plot the course for your future. This involves concretizing your vision into achievable chunks. Start by visualizing what success looks like for you five years, ten years, or even twenty years down the line.

This vision should be a radiant image that excites and puts your heart into overdrive. It should be grand enough to stretch your abilities and yet achievable enough to not dissuade you. To make it palpable, try to visualize it in as much detail as possible. What's the scenery like? Who are the people around you? How are you spending your time? How do you feel? The more brightly you illuminate your vision, the clearer your path will become.

Once this vision is clear, break it down into long-term goals, medium-term goals, and short-term objectives. This methodical segmentation can ensure that your vision is realistic and attainable, as you will be breaking down complex jigsaws into manageable pieces.

4.4. The Master plan: Your Personal Blueprint

Once you have your vision and segmented goals, you can now proceed to forge your personal blueprint. This blueprint is an actionable plan that outlines your objectives, strategies, timelines, and checkpoints.

Your blueprint should consider your strengths to envision and define objectives - careers or personal endeavors that you naturally gravitate toward. It must also include strategies for honing relevant skills, acquiring necessary resources, and seizing the right opportunities.

As a living document, it needs to have flexibility to accommodate changes and unexpected turns of life. Revisit it periodically to make necessary amendments and to reaffirm your commitment to your vision.

4.5. Embracing the Process

Remember, designing your life is not an overnight transformation. It's a continuous, evolving process. Your personal blueprint is not a prison to restrict you, but rather a compass to guide you towards your most fulfilling life. Be patient with yourself and embrace the journey of visioneering your future.

With this invigorating and meticulous process, you would have successfully laid the first stone on your path to creating the life of your dreams!

Chapter 5. Change Catalysts: Embracing Life's Defining Moments

Life is a theater of continuous evolution marked by moments that can shift our trajectory significantly. We label these instances as 'Change Catalysts', pivotal episodes that compel us to look within, reassess our choices, and redesign our paths. We often encounter these moments where we stand at life's intersection, needing to choose which path to tread upon, affecting us profoundly, and inspiring us to cultivate meaningful transformations. This chapter delves into recognizing these critical moments, understanding their quintessence, and harnessing them to usher positivity, growth, and progress.

5.1. The Anatomy of Change Catalysts

Change Catalysts are like seismographs that reflect the magnitude of an impending alteration in your life. These are vital junctures where our mental, emotional, and sometimes physical, responses decide our future. They are discreetly powerful, waging a silent yet colossal impact on our lives. There is no definitive list or fixed profile of change catalysts; they can take myriad forms, ranging from significant life events, such as a career change, moving to a new city, or a life-threatening illness, to subtle stimuli, like a book that shifted your perspective or a casual conversation with a stranger. However, recognizing these catalysts is pivotal to steering your life towards a more fulfilling, enriched, and accomplished existence.

5.2. Identifying Your Change Catalysts

An integral part of navigating Change Catalysts involves recognizing when such life-altering instances occur. Sometimes, it can be a profound personal experience that shakes us to our core. Other times, it could just be a quiet realization leading to a significant internal shift. Identifying these moments requires heightened introspection, emotional intelligence, and willingness to confront reality with unfiltered openness. Acknowledging your Change Catalysts can empower you to address the impediments hindering your growth and grasp the opportunities camouflaged in challenges, thus infusing your life with enriched meaning and wholesome purpose.

5.3. The Significance of Embracing Change Catalysts

Rather than shying away, we should willingly embrace our Change Catalysts, for they are portals that lead to self-evolution. They catalyze our journeys of transformation from the present version of ourselves to an elevated, evolved, and enhanced version. Embracing them may involve stepping into the unknown and braving the storms of discomfort. However, these storms are inevitable rites of passage leading to brilliant rainbows of enlightenment and empowerment. While the storms may be turbulent, the rainbows promise a calm, clear, and confident perspective on life and its many opportunities.

5.4. The Art of Harnessing the Power of Change Catalysts

Harnessing the power of Change Catalysts requires patience,

persistence, and an unflagging belief in your capabilities even in the face of adversity. It involves harnessing these moments as turning points leading you towards a refreshed vision of your life. It necessitates mustering the courage to embrace discomfort, the resilience to rise from setbacks, the determination to persist till the end, and the wisdom to learn from every situation. By subscribing to these practices, you can maximize the transformative potential of these pivotal moments, advancing progressively towards a brighter, bolder, and better future.

5.5. Final Thoughts on Change Catalysts

Change Catalysts carry significant weight in our journey towards self-improvement, growth, and success. Recognizing, embracing, and leveraging these episodes allow us to navigate through life's labyrinth with amplified wisdom, heightened resilience, and a clear vision. They enable us to achieve a state of fluid adaptability, constantly learning, evolving, and growing. In essence, these defining moments form the crucible that forges our true selves, propelling us to the realm of accomplishments, success, and fulfillment. By recognizing and honoring our Change Catalysts, we embark on a transformative journey that elevates our lives to a higher echelon-'The Next Level'.

Approaching life this way, embracing the transformative power of these defining moments, will allow you to grasp every opportunity with both hands, ignite that dormant spark within you, and push the boundaries of the possible and the achievable. Remember, it's not always the destination that matters; the journey - replete with its trials, tribulations, triumphs, and teachings - is equally, if not more, significant. So, seize these moments, maximize their transformative potential, and navigate your path towards a life well-lived!

In conclusion, this chapter underscores the crucial role of Change

Catalysts that can remodel your life, steering you towards triumphs and the attainment of your dreams. This instigating power of yours is all within reach, ready to be harnessed, primed to catapult you towards the life you've always desired. All you need to do is embrace these significant life moments with open arms, understand their transformative power, and leverage that to craft a fulfilling and successful existence that you deserve. Let these enlightening catalysts be your beacon, illuminating a path to your glory and fulfillment.

Chapter 6. Rising from the Rubble: Overcoming Your Past & Building Resilience

Resilience is a powerful force. It's the ability to bounce back in the face of adversity, to stand tall when life topples us down, and to find light amidst profound darkness. Often, it is when we rise from the rubble and conquer our past hardships that we harness the true essence of our inner strength, and it's in these moments that the transformation towards a successful, rewarding life truly begins.

6.1. Embracing Your Past

Our past can be a winding labyrinth, filled with memories of joy, hope, despair, and challenges. Embracing the past means acknowledging it – an authentic acknowledgement which includes the good, the bad, and even the hideous. Understand that what has come to pass was simply an experience, not a determinant of your worth or future. These experiences no longer holds control over your present and future unless you let them. Embrace your past as a treasure trove of lessons, stories and valuable wisdom that fuels your growth and development rather than as an unmanageable baggage of regret and remorse.

To begin, you need to audit your past experiences — both the ones you celebrate and the ones you'd rather forget. Focusing tremendous attention on your past failures and losses can often cloud the potential prosperity awaiting you in the future. Jot down your past experiences, categorize them, and identify which ones uplift you versus which ones tend to drape your emotions in shades of remorse and regret. This might be a painful step, but it's a crucial one.

6.2. Moving Beyond Guilt and Shame

Guilt and shame are two emotions that can keep us anchored to our past, making it difficult to move forward. But we must remember, we are not defined by our mistakes but rather by how we learn from them. We possess the incredible ability to rise above guilt and shame by embracing forgiveness: forgiving ourselves affords us the clarity of mind necessary to see mistakes as a growth opportunity rather than an eternal black mark on our personal record.

Take advantage of this mental schema and remember, every individual on this earth is a work-in-progress constantly learning, growing, and evolving. Guilt and shame may tell you otherwise, but know that they are temporary residents of your emotional residence and have no right to remodel the architecture of your self-esteem.

6.3. Finding Power in Vulnerability

Vulnerability is not a sign of weakness as society often conveys. Instead, it's an emblem of courage – the courage to let your authentic self be seen, heard, and felt. By admitting our vulnerabilities, we allow ourselves the possibility to weather difficult life storms and emerge stronger.

To harness the power of vulnerability, it's important to open up about your struggles. Share your story of hardship and resilience with people you trust — friends, family, mentors, or support groups. By shedding light on our buried fears and anxieties, we disempower them and empower ourselves instead.

6.4. Building Resilience: Tools & Techniques

Rising from the rubble - overcoming your past and building

resilience - isn't an overnight phenomenon, but an ongoing process. However, there are strategies and tools that can foster this resilience within you.

Practices like mindfulness, physical exercise, maintaining a positive attitude, fostering good relationships, and setting realistic goals contribute to building a steadfast resilience. Mindfulness pulls you back into the realm of 'now', breaking the chains of past or future worries. Physical exercise releases stress, clears your mind, and boosts your mood, while a positive attitude helps you see the silver lining in any situation.

Nurturing healthy relationships can be a vital component to resilience-building. Surround yourself with positive, encouraging people who can be your pillars of support during turbulent times. Setting realistic goals, on the other hand, can keep you guided and motivated on your journey to bouncing back.

Taking small yet persistent steps to incorporate these into your life can help you build a robust resilience, thus empowering you to not just beat adversities but also to aim for your life's next level.

6.5. Celebrating Progress

Even as you work on overcoming past traumas and building resilience, it's very important to recognize and celebrate your progress. Celebrations are not limited to grand breakthroughs, even the tiniest steps forward call for happy dances. This not only affirms that you are moving in the right direction but also fuels your motivation to continue the course of your journey, no matter how rough the seas may get.

Rising from the rubble is about nurturing an ongoing relationship with oneself, built on the helix of introspection, acceptance, forgiveness, vulnerability, resilience, and optimism. Overcoming your past, regardless of its density and darkness, and building resilience, regardless of life's adversities, is the way forward. The wisdom from your past is the key that unlocks your future's potential, and resilience is the skill that glues together all the shattered pieces and helps you emerge whole. It is the ingredients of a brilliant, self-constructed antidote to life's uncertainties and a catalyst to catapulting your life to the next level.

Remember, the rubble of your past is not a monument of your failure, but the foundation of your new, invincible castle of resilience.

Chapter 7. Strengthening Your Skillset: Mastering Tools for Success

The journey towards success begins with a thorough understanding of one's capabilities, strengths, and weaknesses. However, recognizing these attributes is merely the first step in a long and demanding process. The core toward reaching your objectives lies in harnessing and strengthening your skillset, utilizing a range of tools designed to propel you to unimaginable heights of accomplishment.

7.1. Dismantling the Skillset Conundrum

When it comes to mastering skills necessary for success, it's crucial to identify what these are and why they're important. Skills range from hard, tangible abilities like programming or proficiency in a second language, to soft skills such as communication and emotional intelligence. Precisely determining which skills are relevant to your particular journey gives you a clear starting point. A concise yet comprehensive list of your essential skills offers a roadmap that eliminates ambiguity from your pathway to success.

7.2. Ascending the Mountain of Mastery

Identifying the skills you require is only part of the battle. Once you know what skills you need, the real task is to master them. This phase requires a significant investment of time, energy, effort, and commitment. Mastery is not an overnight phenomenon; it's a rigorous process that demands persistence and diligence.

Researchers have estimated that achieving mastery in a field requires approximately 10,000 hours of dedicated practice. This is not an arbitrary figure but a testament to the level of commitment and discipline required to excel.

7.3. Tools of the Trade

There is a myriad of tools and resources available that can significantly improve your ability to grasp and harness your skills. These range from traditional choices like books and formal education to modern options such as online courses, digital platforms, and podcasts. Identifying the tools that work best for your learning style and incorporating them into your routine is a major step toward mastery.

7.4. Harnessing Hard Skills

Despite the increasing importance of soft skills, hard skills or technical skills should never be overlooked. Whether you're aiming to become a software developer, a graphic designer, or a scientist, you must take the time to familiarize yourself with the hard skills required for your field. E-learning platforms like Coursera, Udemy, and Khan Academy offer courses in numerous disciplines. They allow for self-paced learning, which means you can absorb knowledge at a speed that suits you.

7.5. Cultivating Soft Skills

Soft skills refer to personal attributes and interpersonal skills that determine how you interact with others. These include aspects like leadership, communication, and emotional intelligence. They may seem less concrete than hard skills but are equally, if not more, important for long-term success. Workshops, seminars, and books can provide knowledge while practical application and reflective practice usher in mastery of these skills.

7.6. The Art of Consistent Learning

Consistency is crucial in the journey towards mastery. Without consistency, even the most ambitious plans fail. Setting a regular learning schedule, committing to it, and tracking your progress is essential. Regular practice, repetition, and application of these skills in everyday life deepens understanding and ingrains these abilities into your psychological makeup, transforming them into second nature.

7.7. Embracing Failure as a Stepping Stone

On the path of mastery, one must anticipate and accept failures and setbacks. It is through mistakes and failures that we learn and improvise. Embracing failure as part of the learning process helps build resilience and persistence, strengthening your mental toughness and equipping you to combat future challenges head-on.

Sculpting a detailed, applicable, and effective skillset takes considerable time, commitment, and energy. However, with consistent and diligent effort, the journey will cultivate not only professional growth but personal development as well, paving the way for a fulfilling life imbued with success. Let this chapter serve as a robust foundation, aiding you in crystallizing your skillset, utilizing the right tools for mastery, and venturing forth towards unrivaled success in your chosen field of endeavor.

Chapter 8. Leaping Out of Your Comfort Zone: Bold Moves, Bolder Outcomes

Stepping out of your comfort zone may seem to be one of the most daunting tasks you may ever have to undertake in life. It involves making the conscious decision to abandon the familiar and safe confines of your current circumstances in order to take bold leaps into areas of uncertainty. Yet, as terrifying as it may sound initially, it's these bold moves that often lead to even bolder outcomes-- outcomes that can catapult you to unprecedented levels of personal and professional success. This chapter will first explore the nature of a comfort zone, lay some strategies to courageously leap out from it, and then delve into what to expect once you do, along with some real-life examples to elucidate these strategies.

8.1. Understanding the Comfort Zone

The comfort zone is a psychological state in which one feels familiar, safe, at ease, and in control. It's encapsulated by a consistent hum of conditions and experiences within which we feel most at home. Being in our comfort zone generally allows us to perform and operate without a sense of risk or threat, whether real or imagined, hence the allure!

Indeed, our comfort zone serves a purpose. It's a space where our activities and behaviors fit a pattern and routine that minimizes stress and risk. This can be beneficial in the short term, allowing us to perform tasks with a level of automaticity that doesn't require much mental effort.

However, our comfort zone can also become a prison, holding us back from testing our abilities or tapping into our hidden potential. Science explains that this comfort zone eventually results in a steady level of performance-- which is another way of saying that if you wish to grow, succeed, and maximize your potential, you must challenge the boundaries of your comfort zone.

8.2. Strategies to Leap Out of Your Comfort Zone

Primarily, understand that embarking on a journey beyond your comfort zone isn't about being reckless or irrational, but about supporting your growth and development. To leap out of your comfort zone, you need a thoughtful approach that combines courage, smart risk taking, and negotiating uncertainty.

\1. **Start Small**: Seeing the comfort zone leap as one huge jump may be overwhelming. Start with minor changes to your routine, tasks you've already mastered, and slowly up the stakes. These small steps can collectively make a big impact and nudge you out of your comfort zone.

\2. **Gradual Exposure**: Voluntarily expose yourself to the things you're afraid of, gradually and consistently. Could it be public speaking, learning a new skill, or just embarking on a new exercise regime? Make it a routine to face these fears.

\3. **Embrace Failure**: Growth is closely intertwined with failure. Embrace it, learn from it, move beyond it. Remember, every failed step is a step closer to success.

\4. **Build up Resilience**: As you step outside your comfort zone, it's important to develop psychological resilience. Take each challenging situation as a way to learn and build up your strength.

\5. **Adopt a Growth Mindset**: A crucial adjunct to leaping out of your comfort zone is adopting a growth mindset, which sees challenges as opportunities for growth rather than insurmountable obstacles.

8.3. Embracing the Bold Outcomes of Bold Moves

Fierce courage often accompanies transcending your comfort zone. As you do, focus on the myriad of rewards it offers; personal growth, resilience, self-confidence, heightened productivity, life satisfaction, and a realm of possibilities.

\1. **Growth**: In terms of personal and professional growth, stepping out of your comfort zone can work miraculous wonders. It incubates creativity, spurs innovation, and catalyzes forward momentum.

\2. **Resilience**: Engaging with what scares us not only helps to vanquish the fears but also fortifies resilience. The more you step outside your comfort zone, the more resilient you will become, ready to face any hurdle life may present.

\3. **Self-confidence**: As you stretch your boundaries and face new challenges, you build self-confidence. Each conquest over fear testifies to your potential, reinforcing your capabilities and boosting your self-confidence.

\4. **Productivity**: Venturing beyond your comfort zone brings about unforeseen challenges. Meeting these challenges head-on increases productivity-- you'll uncover faster, better ways to get things done.

\5. **Life Satisfaction**: People who regularly push their comfort zones are often more content and feel more fulfilled in life. They feel accomplished, successful, and are more likely to meet their own self-expectations.

We see the story of Richard Branson, the founder of Virgin Group, who attributes his success to his willingness to take bold leaps. His famous motto, "Screw it, let's do it" encapsulates the spirit of courageously stepping out of the comfort zone.

In conclusion, your comfort zone is a safe harbor, but no great sailor ever discovered new lands with a ship that never left the harbor. So muster your courage, strap on your shoes, and get ready to leap. Because the world beyond your comfort zone is waiting, and it bears the promise of bolder outcomes. Despite the fear and uncertainty, the leap is necessary and ultimately gratifying. Once you step out, there is no turning back—only an all-encompassing resolve to conquer, thrive, and succeed. So c'mon, dare to leap, for incredible vistas of opportunity lie ahead!

Chapter 9. Recharging Your Drive: Maintaining Motivation Amidst Adversity

In the unfolding of life's intricate tapestry, there exists a complex interplay of events, circumstances, emotions, and experiences, all of which constitute our unique personal journey through the world. Among the most pivotal of these elements is motivation, a vital driving force that not only propels us forward but also, at times, keeps us steadfast amid adversities that inevitably arise along the way. This particular segment delves into the magnitude of maintaining your drive, even in the face of adversity, and provides insight on effective ways to recharge your motivation.

9.1. Setting the Scene: Understanding Motivation

Motivation serves as the propellant that drives us to act. It's an internal psychological construct that stirs our passion, directs our behavior, and influences the decisions we make. Our motivation is influenced by various factors – intrinsic motivations stem from internal rewards and personal satisfaction, while extrinsic motivations originate from external rewards or the avoidance of adverse outcomes. However, when the road gets rocky and adversity hits, maintaining this motivation can become an arduous task. We suddenly find ourselves in a mental quagmire, struggling to fuel our drive and maintain momentum.

9.2. The Impact of Adversity on Our Motivation

Adversities or hardships – in any form and magnitude – can undermine motivation and create psychological hurdles. The stress and anxiety these challenges trigger often lead to reduced mental and physical energy levels. This state can create a self-perpetuating cycle of demotivation, decreased productivity, and further stress. Therefore, it's crucial to acknowledge the potential detrimental impact adversities can have on motivation and to devise strategies that will help maintain our drive even in adverse situations.

9.3. Harnessing the Power of Positivity and Optimism

One potent antidote to adversity-induced demotivation is positivity, exercised through an optimistic outlook on life. Research shows that optimistic individuals tend to be more resilient in the face of adversity, rebounding from challenges faster and more effectively. Positive thinking does not mean ignoring negatives or adopting unrealistic expectations; it's about focusing on opportunities instead of the hurdles, recognizing accomplishments, no matter how small, and fostering gratitude. Cultivating such an attitude helps to recharge your drive and boosts the motivation to tackle challenges head-on.

9.4. Overcoming Obstacles: Strategic Steps to Maintain Motivation

There are several practical steps you can undertake to maintain and recharge your motivational drive, even amid adversity:

1. Identify and refocus on your goals: Remind yourself of why you embarked on this journey in the first place, reaffirm these

intentions and realign your priorities accordingly.

2. Break big tasks into manageable chunks: Overwhelming tasks can drain motivation. Splitting them into smaller, achievable goals can boost productivity, preserving your drive.

3. Lean on supportive networks: Surround yourself with positive individuals who will provide emotional support, encourage your endeavors, and reignite your passion when it wanes.

4. Take care of your physical health: Regular exercise, a balanced diet, and adequate sleep can significantly impact your mental state and thus your motivation.

5. Be kind to yourself: Acknowledge that setbacks are part and parcel of life, and understand that it's okay to stumble. Cultivate self-compassion and patience - they're essential for maintaining motivation amid adversity.

6. Practice mindfulness and meditation: These techniques can help manage stress and anxiety, fostering a relaxation response that fuels a more positive outlook and motivation.

As we remember, motivation is not a constant state; it's an ebb and flow, influenced by various factors, including our current circumstances and how we perceive them. Thus, maintaining motivation in the face of adversity becomes about shifting perception, harnessing positivity, and engaging in strategic actions to recharge our motivational drive, propelling us to overcome obstacles and continue our journey towards success. Just like a car that occasionally runs on low fuel, humans also need recharging to continue their journey persistently. So, buckle up, recharge, maintain your drive and pave the path to triumph.

Chapter 10. Consistency is Key: The Importance of Routine and Persistence

The parable of the turtle and the hare isn't just a childhood fable; it illustrates an age-old truth: victories earned by perseverance and consistency are more enduring. When consistency becomes a part of our mindset, actions, and overall lifestyle, it staves off the uncertainty and imbalance that so easily disrupts our pathway to success.

10.1. Consistency Defined

To foster a complete understanding, it is necessary to first define what consistency really means. Simply put, consistency is the commitment to repeat a set of beneficial behaviors routinely, with minimal variation, over a prolonged period of time. It's easy to do what needs to be done for a day or two, but when days turn into weeks, and weeks turn into months, the struggle to maintain momentum is a reality for most.

A common fallacy is mistaking immediate, sporadic fits of effort for consistency. It is essential to distinguish between the enthusiasm that sprouts when embarking on a new project versus the long-term discipline necessary to see that venture to its fruition. Consistency is more about the journey than any singular moment of triumph. Its power lies in its ability to transform a major goal into a series of small, manageable tasks.

10.2. The Role of Routine in Fostering Consistency

Routines are necessary for fostering consistency. The creation of a schedule, key behaviors, and targeted strategies can fuel our daily persistence. Routines pave a predictable path, and predictability reduces the mental load and apprehension associated with new tasks.

Crafting a routine begins with the identification of critical actions that edge us closer to our goals. The list of tasks need not be lengthy. The magic is not in the number but in the regular repetition. Start by integrating a few essential tasks into your regular schedule and gradually build from there. As the saying goes, "Rome wasn't built in a day" - and neither is our pathway to success.

10.3. Nurturing Persistence

Persistence is the companion that consistency cannot do without. It is the sheer doggedness that keeps us going despite setbacks. To nurture persistence, we must foster patience and dispel the notion that results need to be immediate. The greatest accomplishments are usually realized at the end of long, sometimes arduous, journeys.

Developing a robust support system is pivotal in nurturing persistence. Surrounding ourselves with positive, supportive individuals can provide the motivation we need during tough times. Celebrating small victories is another invaluable strategy to maintain motivation; it reminds us of our potent potential and keeps our spirits high.

10.4. Challenges to Consistency and Overcoming Them

Despite its importance, maintaining consistency can be challenging. Procrastination, distractions, and a lack of immediate results often lead individuals astray from their path of consistency. It is crucial to understand that these obstacles are not permanent roadblocks but hurdles that can be overcome.

Creating an accountable environment is instrumental in overcoming procrastination. For example, a gym partner can contribute to the consistency of your fitness regime. As for distractions, designing a dedicated workspace or a specific working hour can reduce environmental and situational diversions.

10.5. The Rewarding Impact of Consistency - Vibrant Success Stories

There is no dearth of successful individuals accrediting their triumphs to consistency. The co-founder of Twitter, Biz Stone, once said, 'Timing, perseverance, and ten years of trying will eventually make you look like an overnight success.' It is essential to remember that success stories are rarely achieved overnight. They result from dedication, persistence, and the consistent pursuit of a vision.

Developing consistency takes time; it's a repetitive endeavor that harnesses the power of gradual change. As we work on fostering consistency and aligning it with our goals and values, we begin to witness the magic of transformation. And before we know it, what initially seemed like the incremental steps of a turtle have carried us over the finish line. Welcome to the realm of the consistent and persistent, where goals metamorphose into achievements, and dreams translate into reality.

To conclude, consistency, backed by a routine-driven approach and an undying spirit of persistence, is a potent tool that fuels sustainable progress and personal development. Its transformative power lies in its simplicity – never underestimate the potential of the small, consistent steps. They are the keys that unlock the doors to success and the building blocks of monumental achievements. As the saying goes, "Small daily improvements are the key to staggering long-term results."

Chapter 11. Celebrating Milestones: The Sweet Taste of Success & Planning Ahead

Celebrating milestones is integral to the journey of personal growth and triumph. This reflection of past achievements, small or big, not only exudes the sweet taste of success but also prepares us for the challenges to come. Embracing this celebratory spirit not only promotes healthy self-appreciation but also clears our path towards a brighter future.

11.1. The Importance of Celebrating Milestones

Our accomplishments, regardless of their scale, epitomize the embodiment of our efforts, tenacity, and determination. Recognition of these achievements boosts our morale, fostering a positive mindset and self-image. Each triumph is a testament to our strength, and celebrating it paints a vivid picture of progress, resilience, and the immense capacity for growth within us. Celebrations infuse positivity and enthusiasm, energizing us to further our journey and fuel our ambitions with more dedication and zeal.

11.2. Understanding the Sweet Taste of Success

Success tastes sweet, but its essence lies not in the destination reached but rather in the journey undertaken. The endurance, commitment, and resilience summoned along the path shape our character and fortify our spirit. Savoring these victories instills in us a newfound confidence, motivating us to tackle future challenges head on. Hence, the acknowledgement of each mini-success is a celebration of the evolution of our better selves and the realization of our capabilities.

11.3. The Art of Future Planning

Every achievement, when mapped, serves as a stepping stone towards the ascertainment of our ultimate goal. Therefore, planning ahead merits equivalent emphasis. A well-sketched plan offers a clear vision of our desired destination and the obstacles lying on the path. It uncovers the resources required and elucidates the strategies to implement for a seamless navigation through the journey.

11.4. Balancing Celebration with Progression

While it's essential to bask in the glory of our accomplishments, it's equally crucial not to drown in complacency. Maintaining momentum and perpetuating the spirit of progress are key to achieving higher levels of success. Striking a balance between celebrating milestones and nurturing the drive for continuous growth shapes the trajectory of our journey. It's the art of savoring the taste of success while not losing sight of the ultimate goal.

11.5. The Cycle of Success, Celebration, and Planning

In life, success, celebration, and planning exist in a dynamic cycle. Each stage fuels the other and plays a vital role in personal growth and transformation. Success leads to celebration, fostering a heightened sense of self-worth and self-image. Celebration serves as the fuel to accumulate strength for the next leap. Planning then directs this vitality towards actionable objectives, guiding us closer to our ultimate ambitions. This powerful cycle propels us beyond the realms of ordinary and urges us to strive for the extraordinary.

In conclusion, understanding the importance of celebrating milestones, savoring the sweet taste of success, balancing celebration and progression, and understanding the cycle of success, celebration, and planning are all essential aspects of catapulting your life to the next level. It's a potent combination that not only motivates and inspires but also provides a robust framework to shape our future. Embrace the victories, revel in the moments of glory, and continue moving forward with an enlightening vision and robust plan, for the journey towards the pinnacle of success is as spectacular as the view from the top.